father, dear father!

Cartoons by
FRANK EVERS

ABOUT COMICS | CAMARILLO, CALIFORNIA

Father, Dear Father!
Originally published by Abbey Books, 1958
About Comics edition published September, 2018

ISBN-13: 978-1-936404-94-0

Customized editions are available.

Send all queries to *questions@aboutcomics.com*

"What a lucky guy, it's the third time he's
had a virous this term."

"Can you spare Jimmy for the day
Mrs. Coogan? We've got important business."

"I can't afford fancy lures Father, so I stick
to plain worms."

"COOGAN!"

"Same old trouble Father, biliouness from bills."

"Looks like they cleaned out the church
basement at last."

"That's good aged lemonade Father, it's
two weeks old."

"Calling them like that is no venial sin, Father."

"Guess what I got for my birthday."

"Smoke up men, I've just become an uncle."

"I don't know how I got up here myself, Father."

"Oh boy, what penances he'll dish out today!"

1.

2.

"Okay men, check your weapons and get into working togs, Mass begins in five minutes."

"Might as well tell me now, we have confessions tomorrow anyhow."

"He's been putting on since that talent scout
moved into our parish."

"Anybody see my chocolate coated
anti-biotic pills?"

"Lucky fer you I always respect a
man's uniform."

23

"You should have brought a bigger apple."

"Just as we were coming out of the red."

"The game went twelve innings, you know
how it is, Father."

"COOGAN!"

"HOWDY SHERIFF! Why–er–I mean
–hello Bishop !"

"What crazy hats some women wear nowadays."

1.

2.

5.

6.

3.

4.

7.

8.

"Now that there's no one around let's hear
how a little Dixieland sounds on that thing."

"Can't use it! Surely Father, there must be some
broken down millionaire around."

"Let's shut one eye, they're nice to us
when we're remiss."

"Patience Father, just sixty seconds and Lent
will be over."

"Now if you fellows can get up thirty-seven cents
we may be able to bail him out."

"Good-bye angel cake!"

"What a break Father, you've just won
one dozen fancy plaid sport shirts."

"I just told him my name is Eve, offered him this apple and away he ran."

"Pin it right there Father, the picture is perfect."

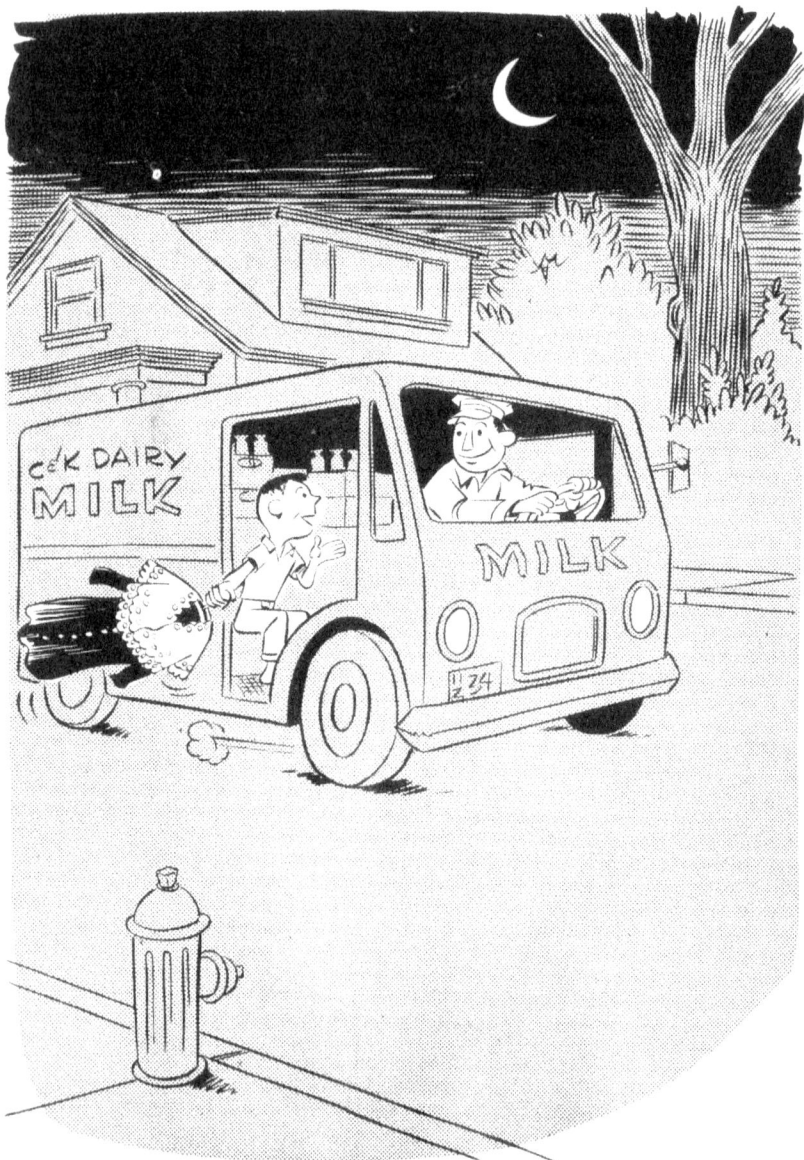

"Hope you don't mind Mr. Dugan, I drew the
early shift this week."

1.

2.

GIANT
SKY
ROCKET

5.

6.

3

4.

7.

8

"There's nothing to worry about, it's
only up to my ankles."

"Nice fielding, Father."

"Get me out of here, Father."

"Which reminds me, I've got to go to my
music teacher tomorrow."

"I can't damage it Father, the man on TV said
it's water-proof upholstery."

"Don't mind him Father, I'm training him like
Lassie and that's his first trick."

"What's cookin' inside, Doc?"

"We've got a new rythm. Wanna hear it, Father?"

"I ordered two dozen oranges and
ONE water-melon."

"You know that little valve you told me not to
touch? Well I touched it, Father."

"COOGAN!"

"Come on up fellers, this feels good
on the feet."

"I have an old Aunt who is crazy about the stuff."

"Are you sure he never played this game before?"

"The crystal ball says you will play a big part in future heavenly travel."

"How about a little change of pace, Father?"

"You said we needed firewood, didn't you?"

"Hold your fire men, top brass approaching."

"COOGAN!"

"Somebody back there isn't pulling his weight."

" 'nuff for today, men."

"Better treat my visitor first."

"Can I come in when you start to serve the
coffee and cake?"

"Got any liniment home, Father?"

"Anybody like a well, well done one?"

"*Psst!* Have you seen today's *Daily Nun*??"

www.ingramcontent.com/pod-product-compliance
Lightning Source LLC
Chambersburg PA
CBHW071848020426
42331CB00007B/1911